MW00611025

# MYSTIC

# MONDAYS

## TAROT JOURNAL

**YOUR GUIDE TO UNLOCKING
THE TRANSFORMATIVE
POWER OF TAROT**

Grace Duong

CHRONICLE BOOKS

SAN FRANCISCO

ISBN 978-1-7972-2528-9

Manufactured in China.

Design by Henna Crowner.

10 9 8 7 6 5 4 3 2 1

Chronicle books and gifts are available at special quantity discounts to corporations, professional associations, literacy programs, and other organizations. For details and discount information, please contact our premiums department at corporatesales@chroniclebooks.com or at 1-800-759-0190.

Chronicle Books LLC
680 Second Street
San Francisco, California 94107
www.chroniclebooks.com

# Contents

0. THE FOOL

# Introduction

Welcome to the Mystic Mondays universe!

Diving into tarot is a dive into your subconscious. As you study the cards, your journey with yourself will expand, and your self-awareness will grow as you begin to recognize your strengths and shadows. Often a tarot reading confirms exactly what is going on in our lives. The tarot cards just know. They are a portal to connect with your higher self, ancestors, guides, and anyone else on your spiritual team. Through using the tarot cards, you develop a language to speak to the divinity that lives within you.

This tarot journal is designed to be used alongside your cards. If you're here, you are likely familiar with Mystic Mondays Tarot, a vibrant tarot deck for the modern mystic. When I created the deck, I felt a calling to make tarot fun, friendly, and accessible while tapping into the healing power of highly saturated color frequencies and bold, geometric shapes. I wanted the art of Mystic Mondays to get to the heart of the matter so that anyone, beginner and expert alike, could approach using tarot without getting intimidated. Before I created *Mystic Mondays*, I couldn't fully resonate with any deck out there. I couldn't find one that really spoke to me and represented my present-day experience, and I figured others probably felt the same way. Now, it has become a line of tarot, oracle, and other products that make up the magical world of Mystic Mondays with the mission of empowering you to craft your own inner magic, reminding you of what was always there to begin with.

This journal is meant to hold space for that inner magic—all the thoughts and inklings and discoveries that emerge as you journey through the deck. Even though the cards have common meanings, we all can interpret them in different ways because of our unique experiences as individuals. As part of the collective, we can gain the general meaning of the card, but as individuals we approach our tarot practice through the filter of our own experiences. That is why, as the tarot reader, you hold a special key for unlocking the meanings of the cards for yourself. You have your own way of approaching reading the cards. There is no right or wrong way to do it! It's just your way.

The power of tarot lies in its imagery and in the symbolism that the images carry. Although tarot has 78 cards, depending on the artist the stylistic depiction of each card can be different. As you study different cards and different decks, look at the color choices, lines, shapes, and other artistic decisions. Different decks have different personalities! You might pull out specific decks for certain occasions and resonate with one over another. The mood of the deck can influence its persona and the tone of voice that it carries. As you'd choose a friend for your inner circle, choose your decks wisely! You'll notice the ones you are drawn to and relate to the most.

Think of your tarot deck as an ally to guide you closer to your intuitive voice. The point of connecting to intuitive tools like tarot is to help empower you to trust yourself more deeply. Too often we are misguided by the external world of advertisements, social media, news, and other factors that take away from our inner truth: that we are enough and have all the resources within ourselves. The journey is to learn to trust your intuition and to trust your inner voice.

This tarot journal helps you to connect with and explore that inner voice, and ultimately, discover your truth. The pages are designed so that you can record all the synchronicities, affirmations, and other wisdoms in one place. Committing to this journaling practice will help you boost your confidence as a tarot reader and increase your self-knowledge as you begin to recognize your patterns, habits, beliefs, and triggers. As you log your entries, they will become a record of your evolution. The Mystic Mondays Tarot Journal is here to guide and support you through this transformation! Here's what you'll discover in the following pages:

✳ **Tarot Overview Guide:** This easy-to-follow guide will give you a brief introduction to tarot and significant categories within the deck, along with a bit of guidance on common meanings for each card.

✳ **Card Meanings:** What do the cards mean to you? In this section, you will record keywords and correspondences, and reflect more deeply on each card, creating your own personal tarot reference guide.

✳ **Tarot Spreads:** Use this space to record all your favorite tarot spreads and as inspiration to create your own once you grow more comfortable with your practice!

✳ **Tarot Readings:** Practice makes perfect! In this space, you'll be able to log your tarot readings through drawings and notes. Two layouts are available: single pages for smaller spreads and double pages for more extensive readings.

You'll also find a Tools and Resources section at the end of the journal with space to record all the physical and digital resources that enhance your tarot practice, including your decks, your tarot community, and more. And for additional tarot resources, inspiration, and materials, you can visit www.mysticmondays.com or download the Mystic Mondays app. Thank you for being here and for being a part of our cosmic collective!

—*Grace Duong, creator of Mystic Mondays*

# Tarot Overview

Tarot is traditionally a system of 78 cards. Each card contains an upright meaning and a reversed meaning when the card is read upside down. That means there are potentially 156 meanings within one deck (though it's worth noting that not all decks include reversed descriptions, and not all tarot readers read reversals—more on this on page 33).

When cards are paired with one another in multi-card displays (called spreads), there are even more possible interpretations of what the tarot cards are communicating—which can easily overwhelm beginners and advanced readers alike. The goal is to get comfortable with each card and develop your relationship with them so that you are not just reciting a memorization of what the card means, but channeling information from a place of intuition. This is where the self-trust comes in—you innately know what these cards mean, and the messages coming through are exactly what you (or if you are conducting a reading for another person, what they) need at this exact moment.

However, having a solid foundation of what the cards mean can help you access that point of intuition, especially when you start to use other decks in your practice! It's easy to second-guess yourself when there is so much information out there. Spending some introspection time with each card will help you solidify what the card means to you with practice and repetition. When you draw a card, this journal will help you record your meanings from a place of truth, defining your relationship to that card so that you remember the meaning based on your personal experiences.

Here you'll find some foundational information to get you started on your journey.

# Major Arcana

Major Arcana cards are numbered from 0 to 21, beginning with the Fool at 0, which indicates unlimited possibilities, and ending with the World at 21, which indicates completion. The journey from the Fool to the World is often related to a hero's journey, with the progression through the cards showing up as life's challenges, triumphs, and revelations. This journey is associated with your soul's evolution and spiritual growth.

| 0. THE FOOL | |
|---|---|
| 🪐 URANUS | |
| ▲ UPRIGHT | ▼ REVERSED |
| Free Spirit | Foolish |
| Purity | Careless |
| Beginnings | Naive |

| I. THE MAGICIAN | |
|---|---|
| 🪐 MERCURY | |
| ▲ UPRIGHT | ▼ REVERSED |
| Inventive | Trickery |
| Manifestation | Manipulation |
| True Potential | Untapped Potential |

| II. THE HIGH PRIESTESS | |
|:---:|:---:|
| MOON | |
| ▲ UPRIGHT | ▼ REVERSED |
| Intuition | Reconnect |
| Serenity | Neglect |
| Divine Goddess | Secrets |

| III. THE EMPRESS | |
|:---:|:---:|
| VENUS | |
| ▲ UPRIGHT | ▼ REVERSED |
| Goddess | Dependence |
| Femininity | Attachment |
| Mother Earth | Fruitless |

| IV. THE EMPEROR | |
|:---:|:---:|
| ARIES | |
| ▲ UPRIGHT | ▼ REVERSED |
| Authority | Tyranny |
| Ambition | Domination |
| Power | Headstrong |

| V. THE HIEROPHANT ||
|---|---|
| ⊘ TAURUS ||
| ▲ UPRIGHT | ▼ REVERSED |
| Conventional | Rebel |
| Institution | Maverick |
| Tradition | Confinement |

| VI. THE LOVERS ||
|---|---|
| ⊘ GEMINI ||
| ▲ UPRIGHT | ▼ REVERSED |
| Love | Imbalance |
| Alignment | Misalignment |
| Choices | Differences |

| VII. THE CHARIOT ||
|---|---|
| ⊘ CANCER ||
| ▲ UPRIGHT | ▼ REVERSED |
| Victory | Directionless |
| Willpower | Off-Course |
| Inner Drive | Roaming |

| VIII. STRENGTH | |
|---|---|
| 🪐 LEO | |
| ▲ UPRIGHT | ▼ REVERSED |
| Fierce | Apprehensive |
| Endurance | Doubtful |
| Courage | Anxious |

| IX. THE HERMIT | |
|---|---|
| 🪐 VIRGO | |
| ▲ UPRIGHT | ▼ REVERSED |
| Soul-Searching | Loneliness |
| Reflection | Confinement |
| Truth | Withdrawal |

| X. THE WHEEL OF FORTUNE | |
|---|---|
| 🪐 JUPITER | |
| ▲ UPRIGHT | ▼ REVERSED |
| Change | Unfortunate Events |
| Fate | Resisting Change |
| Karma | Letting Go |

| XI. JUSTICE | |
|---|---|
| 🪐 LIBRA | |
| ▲ UPRIGHT | ▼ REVERSED |
| Law | Injustice |
| Objective | Unfair |
| Fair | Delinquency |

| XII. THE HANGED WOMAN | |
|---|---|
| 🪐 NEPTUNE | |
| ▲ UPRIGHT | ▼ REVERSED |
| Sacrifice | Avoidance |
| Patience | Sacrifice |
| Suspension | Delay |

| XIII. DEATH | |
|---|---|
| 🪐 SCORPIO | |
| ▲ UPRIGHT | ▼ REVERSED |
| Change | Fear |
| Ending | Uncertainty |
| Rebirth | Resisting Change |

| XIV. TEMPERANCE | |
|---|---|
|  SAGITTARIUS | |
| ▲ UPRIGHT | ▼ REVERSED |
| Balance | Imbalance |
| Patience | Discord |
| Synergy | Frustration |

| XV. THE DEVIL | |
|---|---|
|  CAPRICORN | |
| ▲ UPRIGHT | ▼ REVERSED |
| Addiction | Awareness |
| Enslavement | Breaking Free |
| Fears | Empowerment |

| XVI. THE TOWER | |
|---|---|
| MARS | |
| ▲ UPRIGHT | ▼ REVERSED |
| Destruction | Warning |
| Abrupt Change | Fear of Change |
| Lightning | Avoidance |

| XVII. THE STAR | |
| --- | --- |
|  AQUARIUS | |
| ▲ UPRIGHT | ▼ REVERSED |
| Healing<br>Inspiration<br>Serenity | Uninspired<br>In the Dark<br>Adrift |

| XVIII. THE MOON | |
| --- | --- |
|  PISCES | |
| ▲ UPRIGHT | ▼ REVERSED |
| Surreal<br>Subconscious<br>Shadow Self | Confusion<br>Mixed Signals<br>Hazy |

| XIX. THE SUN | |
| --- | --- |
|  SUN | |
| ▲ UPRIGHT | ▼ REVERSED |
| Positive Vibes<br>Warmth<br>Radiance | Lackluster<br>Cloudy<br>Unrealistic |

| XX. JUDGEMENT | |
|---|---|
| PLUTO | |
| ▲ UPRIGHT | ▼ REVERSED |
| Absolution | Absolution |
| Evaluation | Evaluation |
| Reflection | Reflection |

| XXI. THE WORLD | |
|---|---|
| SATURN | |
| ▲ UPRIGHT | ▼ REVERSED |
| Completion | Final Stretch |
| Achievement | Impediment |
| Unity | Hindrance |

# Minor Arcana

The Minor Arcana suits—Cups, Pentacles, Swords, and Wands—represent everyday life occurrences. Each Minor Arcana card correlates to a number, which can relate to the meanings in numerology. Each suit starts off with an Ace card (which signifies the number one), followed by two through ten. The Court cards—Princess, Knight, Queen, and King—are numbered from 11 through 14, in succession of the Court cards hierarchy.

**WATER**

Emotions

Intuition

Relationships

Water Signs

♋ Cancer

♏ Scorpio

♓ Pisces

## CUPS

Cups represent emotions, intuition, and relationships. They speak to your inner states and your ability to connect with yourself and others—basically anything to do with the affairs of the heart. Cups can be very soothing, healing, and cleansing, depending on the refreshment your cup card is offering!

Some characteristics of the Cups suit are refreshing, dreamy, intuitive, psychic, creative, and imaginative. On the flip side, Cups can also represent distortion, living in a fantasy, unrealistic expectations, emotional blocks, and repression.

▲ **UPRIGHT**
Creativity
Emotional Expression
Free Flow

▼ **REVERSED**
Release
Emotional Exhaustion
Repression

**ACE**

▲ **UPRIGHT**
Partnership
Complementary Duality

▼ **REVERSED**
Breakup
Clash
Disconnect

**TWO**

▲ **UPRIGHT**

Celebration

Squad Goals

Community

▼ **REVERSED**

Conformity

Affair

People Pleasing

**THREE**

▲ **UPRIGHT**

Distracted

Withdrawal

Rumination

▼ **REVERSED**

Stubborn

Self-Absorption

Lost
Opportunities

**FOUR**

▲ **UPRIGHT**

Disappointment

Setback

Perspective

▼ **REVERSED**

Forgiveness

Emotional
Maturity

Recovery

**FIVE**

▲ **UPRIGHT**

Familiarity

Innocence

Nostalgia

▼ **REVERSED**

Rose-Colored
Glasses

Idealistic

Childhood
Trauma

**SIX**

▲ **UPRIGHT**

Illusion

Prizes

Temptation

▼ **REVERSED**

Fantasy

Escapism

Diversion

**SEVEN**

▲ **UPRIGHT**

Introspection

Deeper Purpose

Brooding

▼ **REVERSED**

Avoidance

Paralyzing

Indecisive

**EIGHT**

▲ **UPRIGHT**

Wish Come True

Fulfillment

Pleasures

▼ **REVERSED**

Overindulgence

Impatience

Unrealistic
Expectations

**NINE**

▲ **UPRIGHT**

Wholeness

Connection

Full Circle

▼ **REVERSED**

Broken Family

Disjointed

Blocked
Intimacy

**TEN**

▲ **UPRIGHT**

Flow

Synchronicity

Mystic
Messages

▼ **REVERSED**

Low Tides

Immaturity

Emotional
Instability

**PRINCESS**

▲ **UPRIGHT**

Romantic

Emotional
Elation

Adoration

▼ **REVERSED**

Moody

Emotional
Overload

Reactive

**KNIGHT**

▲ **UPRIGHT**

Intuition

Compassion

Open Heart

▼ **REVERSED**

Restriction

Delusion

Overemotional

**QUEEN**

▲ **UPRIGHT**

Equilibrium

Mindfulness

Humanity

▼ **REVERSED**

Emotional
Abuse

Toxic

Low Spirits

**KING**

## EARTH

Finances

Materials

Physical

Earth Signs

♉ Taurus

♍ Virgo

♑ Capricorn

# PENTACLES

Pentacles is associated with the Earth element, giving this suit a grounding and sturdy presence. On an esoteric level, the Pentacles can also relate to your roots—like connecting to your ancestors and legacy, the story you're crafting for yourself and future generations. It can also pertain to the ego and physical self-image.

Some characteristics of the Pentacles suit are hard-working, grounded, practical, loyal, and stable. On the flip side, Pentacles can also represent traits such as being stubborn, boring, materialistic, unable to adapt, and rigid.

ACE

▲ UPRIGHT
Abundance
Manifestation
Prosperity

▼ REVERSED
Money Mishaps
Reevaluation
Financial
Hardships

TWO

▲ UPRIGHT
Balance
Prioritization
Daily Affairs

▼ REVERSED
Financial
Instability
Neglect
Disorganization

THREE

▲ UPRIGHT
Teamwork
Collaboration
Synergy

▼ REVERSED
Challenge
Power Struggle
Competition

FOUR

▲ UPRIGHT
Control
Stability
Conservative

▼ REVERSED
Materialism
Selfish
Frugality

▲ **UPRIGHT**
Abandonment
Misfortune
Loss

▼ **REVERSED**
Financial
Recovery
Perseverance
Rebuilding
Wealth

**FIVE**

▲ **UPRIGHT**
Giving and
Receiving
Flow
Prosperity

▼ **REVERSED**
Greed
Being Taken
Advantage Of
Debt

**SIX**

▲ **UPRIGHT**
Patience
Investment
Sustainability

▼ **REVERSED**
Wasted Effort
Restructuring
Low Return

**SEVEN**

▲ **UPRIGHT**
Hustle
Grit
Craftsmanship

▼ **REVERSED**
Self-Judgement
Impatience
Perfectionism

**EIGHT**

▲ **UPRIGHT**
True Colors
Splendor
Vitality

▼ **REVERSED**
Self-Sabotage
Materialistic
Dependency

**NINE**

▲ **UPRIGHT**
Communal
Support
Wealth
Legacy

▼ **REVERSED**
Financial Ruin
Blame
Destruction

**TEN**

▲ **UPRIGHT**
Thirst for
Knowledge
Grounded
Practical

▼ **REVERSED**
Daydreaming
Delays
Complacency

**PRINCESS**

▲ **UPRIGHT**
Harvest
Dedication
Routine

▼ **REVERSED**
Bored
Tedium
Apathy

**KNIGHT**

▲ **UPRIGHT**
Earth Mother
Nourishment
Hearth

▼ **REVERSED**
Workaholic
Smothering
Isolation

**QUEEN**

▲ **UPRIGHT**
Attainment
Prosperity
Abundance

▼ **REVERSED**
Arrogant
Egotistical
Closefisted

**KING**

## AIR

Knowledge

Mental Pursuits

Communication

Air Signs

♊ Gemini

♎ Libra

♒ Aquarius

# SWORDS

Swords is associated with the Air element, giving this suit an intellectual, curious, and perceptive quality. It revolves around the fortress of the mind, our perception, the way we think, how we process information, and planning and executing strategy. Like the wind, air can carry information with grace and ease or as forcefully as a tornado.

Some characteristics of the Swords suit are original, dynamic, witty, intelligent, and balanced. On the flip side, Swords can also represent traits like being detached, condescending, cold-hearted, blunt, and "head-in-the-clouds" idealistic.

**▲ UPRIGHT**
Clarity
Pure Power
Breakthrough

**▼ REVERSED**
Confusion
Headcase
Disarray

ACE

**▲ UPRIGHT**
Impasse
Stillness
Indecision

**▼ REVERSED**
Dispute
Indecision
Mental Overload

TWO

**▲ UPRIGHT**
Heartbreak
Rejection
Pain

**▼ REVERSED**
Releasing Pain
Healing Heart
Forgiveness

THREE

**▲ UPRIGHT**
Recharge
Savasana
Rest

**▼ REVERSED**
Depletion
Burnout
Exhaustion

FOUR

▲ **UPRIGHT**

Self-Interest

Conquest

Survival Mode

▼ **REVERSED**

Forgive and Forget

Amend

Conflict

**FIVE**

▲ **UPRIGHT**

Transition

Migration

Letting Go

▼ **REVERSED**

Resistance

Stuck

Stagnation

**SIX**

▲ **UPRIGHT**

Deception

Discreet

Secrets

▼ **REVERSED**

Escape

Clearing Conscience

Reveal

**SEVEN**

▲ **UPRIGHT**

Limitation

Confinement

Restriction

▼ **REVERSED**

Awakening

Liberation

Open to Change

**EIGHT**

▲ **UPRIGHT**

Anxiety

Worry

Distress

▼ **REVERSED**

Mindfulness

Conscious Choices

Thought Patterns

**NINE**

▲ **UPRIGHT**

Betrayal

Fatality

Backstabbed

▼ **REVERSED**

Victimhood

Restoration

Transformation

**TEN**

▲ **UPRIGHT**

Inquisitive

Verbose

Lively

▼ **REVERSED**

Contrarian

Annoyance

Motormouth

**PRINCESS**

▲ **UPRIGHT**

Intense Focus

Radical

Obsessive

▼ **REVERSED**

Impatient

Impulsive

Reckless

**KNIGHT**

▲ **UPRIGHT**

Clear

Meticulous

Intellectual

▼ **REVERSED**

Ice Queen

Judgemental

Detached

**QUEEN**

▲ **UPRIGHT**

Clarity

Mental Strength

Cerebral

▼ **REVERSED**

Mental Abuse

Power Hungry

Manipulative

**KING**

FIRE

Passions

Creativity

Spiritual
Connection

Fire Signs

♈ Aries

♌ Leo

♐ Sagittarius

## WANDS

Wands are conduits of magic, with both the power to create and the power to destroy. Wands can point to our mindset and our intention. Much of what we think we are capable of is what we believe. Our thoughts inform our actions. By freeing ourselves of our limiting thoughts, we also give ourselves the keys to our highest potential.

Some characteristics of the Wands suit are driven, passionate, optimistic, energetic, and creative. On the flip side, Wands can also represent traits like being self-centered, arrogant, overly dramatic, rash, and immature.

▲ UPRIGHT
Illumination
Inspiration
Pure Potential

▼ REVERSED
Vague
Ambiguous
Irresolute

ACE

▲ UPRIGHT
Advance
Explore
Prospects

▼ REVERSED
Doubt
Limitations
Comfort Zone

TWO

▲ UPRIGHT
Persistence
Anticipation
Progression

▼ REVERSED
Barriers
Poor Planning
Obstacle

THREE

▲ UPRIGHT
Home
Backbone
Foundation

▼ REVERSED
Instability
Uncertainty
Flightiness

FOUR

▲ **UPRIGHT**
Competition
Diversity
Rivalry

▼ **REVERSED**
Avoid Conflict
Compromise
Truce

**FIVE**

▲ **UPRIGHT**
Victory
Validation
Acknowledg-
ement

▼ **REVERSED**
Apprehensive
Rebuild
Reputation

**SIX**

▲ **UPRIGHT**
Attack
Challenge
Stand Ground

▼ **REVERSED**
Territorial
Loss of Power
Overwhelm

**SEVEN**

▲ **UPRIGHT**
Progress
Movement
Rapid Action

▼ **REVERSED**
Rush
Impatience
Urgency

**EIGHT**

▲ **UPRIGHT**
Wisdom
Perseverance
Last Stretch

▼ **REVERSED**
Claustrophobic
Resentment
Tentative

**NINE**

▲ **UPRIGHT**
Duty
Responsibility
Obligation

▼ **REVERSED**
Martyr
Resentment
Heaviness

**TEN**

▲ **UPRIGHT**
Creative
Expression
Spark
Free Spirit

▼ **REVERSED**
Deflation
Freedom to Fail
Learning
Experience

**PRINCESS**

▲ **UPRIGHT**
Ambition
Risk-Taker
Action-
Oriented

▼ **REVERSED**
Impatience
Carelessness
Rashness

**KNIGHT**

▲ **UPRIGHT**
Vivacious
Dynamic
Authenticity

▼ **REVERSED**
Intrusive
Contentious
Dejection

**QUEEN**

▲ **UPRIGHT**
Natural Leader
Visionary
Entrepreneur

▼ **REVERSED**
Shrewd
Dictatorial
Domineering

**KING**

# Court Cards

## PRINCESSES
Beginner Stages, Learning, Exploration

## KNIGHTS
Taking Action, Plan in Motion, Using Learned Skills

## QUEENS
Leads with Inner Power, Confidence, Maturity

## KINGS
Leads with Outer Power, Mastery, Authority

The Court cards are expressed as members of a royal family—Princesses, Knights, Queens, and Kings (in some decks, the Princess is referred to as the Page). The Court cards can indicate a level of maturity or experience, with Princesses and Knights viewed as younger and Queens and Kings as older. The Court cards can also be viewed as levels of mastery, with Princesses as the beginner stages of attaining a new skill related to that suit, and Kings as the mastery of the lessons of that suit. You can look at the Court cards, like the numbered Minor Arcana cards, as a progression, with each Court card representing a new level and attainment of self within that suit.

The Court cards can also indicate where you are currently in your life. For example, the Princess of Pentacles could represent the part of you that is learning tangible skills that you could apply to your life and could show that you are at the early stages of learning those skills.

Lastly, the Court cards can represent different people in your life who embody the characteristics of that card. A good way to forge a deeper connection with the Court cards is to lay them out in front of you and assign each card a person you know in your life whom you associate with the card's traits. That might help you create a stronger tie to the card and help you remember what the card indicates each time it appears in a reading.

# Numerology

| ONE |
| --- |
| New Beginnings, Potential, Opportunities |

| TWO |
| --- |
| Balance, Partnership, Duality |

| THREE |
| --- |
| Collaboration, Groups, Growth |

| FOUR |
| --- |
| Structure, Stability, Foundation |

| FIVE |
| --- |
| Change, Instability, Conflict |

| SIX |
| --- |
| Communication, Flow, Harmony |

| SEVEN |
| --- |
| Reflection, Introspection, Assessment |

| EIGHT |
| --- |
| Mastery, Progression, Awareness |

| NINE |
| --- |
| Attainment, Transition, Almost at the End |

| TEN |
| --- |
| Cycle Ending, Renewal, Full Circle |

Numerology is the study of the symbolism and spiritual significance of numbers. Tarot cards are associated with specific numbers, and we can apply numerology to tarot to see patterns and learn correspondences.

The numerology chart shown here relates to the numbers in the Minor Arcana. In the Minor Arcana, the numbers run from one to ten in each suit (with Aces being equivalent to one). One indicates the beginning of a cycle, journey, or goal, and ten indicates the end of a cycle or the attainment of a goal. Once you are comfortable with reading the Minor Arcana cards and numerology, you can start to draw patterns and see parallels between the themes of the Major Arcana cards that carry the same number. For example, Aces can relate to the themes of the Magician card, which signifies inventiveness, true potential, and manifestation.

Although they are less commonly used with numerology, Court cards are associated with the numbers 11 to 14 (beginning with the Princess and progressing to the King), and similarly, can relate to the themes associated with that number in the Major Arcana. For example, the Princess is equivalent to 11 in numerology, and in the Major Arcana XI is Justice.

As you learn to apply numerology to tarot, you can add another layer of meaning to your readings. For example, if you know that five indicates change, instability, and conflict, and that Pentacles is associated with finances, materials, and the physical world, you can extrapolate layers of meaning when you pull a Five of Pentacles.

I. THE MAGICIAN

# Card Meanings

In this section, you will find images of every tarot card, along with space to compile your thoughts about each card. Tracking all your insights and reflections will allow a process of discovery, bringing you closer to what rings truest for your experience of the card. After all, you are approaching each card from a completely different lens, so even if you were to read and learn from a book and memorize the meanings, it would not be quite the same as listening to your intuition.

## How to Interpret Each Card

To interpret a card, begin by tapping into your senses. What feeling are you getting from the card? Look at the imagery, the colors, and the overall tone. From there, you can begin to craft a story and perhaps even relate it to a memory, person, place, or thing that the card reminds you of.

Now, look at the details. What symbols and subject matter are present in this card? Do they appear anywhere else in the deck? By connecting icons and imagery in the deck to one another, you begin to draw patterns between cards that can be related. Perhaps the color blue is present in certain cards and evokes a certain feeling in you.

As you're tapping into your senses, evoke the detective, the researcher, and the librarian within you to go even deeper. Feel free to look up meanings from multiple sources as you gather information, edit, and refine what card meaning feels truest for you. Ask questions and be open to the answers!

You can also look at each card from a personal perspective. When you relate a card to a memory, a dear person (or people) in your life, and/or a favorite place it can all help you develop a relationship with the card that feels more personal. This way of relating to the cards can also help you remember the card's meaning from a place of innate knowing rather than memorization. The card becomes familiar, like a fated friend. This gives your readings that special sauce, a divine message from your spiritual team.

Notice how the dialogue flows between you and the cards—some cards may easily give you messages and some cards may be a bit harder to interpret. Ask yourself why you relate to certain cards over others. Allow time and space to fill in the blanks if answers are not coming immediately. Sometimes the cards don't immediately reveal all their secrets and it can take a period of time to feel like you know the card very well. Have patience with the process! And most importantly, have patience with yourself.

# 10 Activities for Connecting to the Cards

Below you'll find some ideas for ways you can connect to the cards more deeply, which will help you discover how each card speaks to you. You can always come back to these activities to gain clarity as your tarot journey continues to evolve and unfold.

1.   Make a "good" and "bad" pile of cards. This is based on pure intuition and is an activity based on pure instinct. Start with a deck of cards in one pile. Turn over each card and quickly place it in either a "good" pile if it resonates with you, and a "bad" pile if it doesn't. This simple and quick activity can give you insight into how you relate to each card based on your instincts.

2.   Lay out all the cards by categories:

   ✴ **Major Arcana**

   ✴ **Cups Suit**

   ✴ **Pentacles Suit**

   ✴ **Swords Suit**

   ✴ **Wands Suit**

   From a bird's-eye view, seeing the cards side-by-side in chronological order can allow you to see patterns that appear throughout the deck and start to see the similarities and differences between the cards. You can begin to discover patterns between cards that seem similar in subject matter, iconography, color, and tone and also identify the differences between cards.

3. Meditate with the card and ask for it to reveal its messages to you. Find a quiet space and play a relaxing song. Set an intention to connect with that card. As an example, the intention can be something like this: "For today's meditation, I connect to the ___ card. I ask for you to share any messages with me. I open up my channels to receive these messages. Thank you!" You might be surprised at the revelations that come up! Remember to record your revelations inside this journal.

4. Write a story about each card as if the cards were characters. Follow the five W's: who, what, when, where, and why. In a storyline, how would these archetypes interact with one another? What is their relationship to one another? Think about the Greek gods and goddesses and their relationships. What would this look like in the tarot world? Feel free to let your imagination go wild as you construct this narrative! Let it be an exercise to connect more deeply with the archetypes of the cards and how they can relate to one another.

5. Write a dialogue as if you and the card are speaking to each other. Grab a blank piece of paper and, as if you are writing a script, start off with your name and pose a question. Example:

   ✳ **YOUR NAME:** Ask the card a question

   ✳ **CARD:** Response

   Continue this dialogue until you feel the activity is complete, but it is recommended to carve out at least 15 minutes so you can really connect with the card. You can even try writing your dialogue with your dominant hand, and writing the card's dialogue in your nondominant hand. Your nondominant hand is usually the hand of your subconscious mind. If you want to take it a step further, you can also use different pen colors to really show the different tone of voice you and your card represent!

6. Take the tarot card on a date! Some people like to take a special card while traveling, putting it inside their wallet, book, phone case, purse, or other place to really feel the energy of the card and its meaning while they're out and about. You can try it and see how you feel with that tarot card accompanying you on your trip. It can be as simple as going to the grocery store or to the movies. The point is to see if you feel a difference between having the tarot card with you and not having the card with you. Notice if you feel a change in the energy that surrounds you that day. Write about your experience in this journal!

7. Pull a daily card every day and journal about how the energy of the card is showing up for you that day. That way, you can connect deeply with one card on a daily basis. If you're on the go, be sure to draw your card on the Mystic Mondays app! Then, you can reflect on your tarot and oracle cards no matter where you are.

8. Pick a tarot spread and see if you can interpret the meanings without looking at a guidebook. You can start with just three cards and gradually work your way up. See page 137 for a list of spreads you can use. When you finish placing your cards according to the spread you chose, look at the imagery and see if you notice any patterns. Tap into the storyteller inside of you! Record your discoveries in this journal in the "Spreads" section.

9.	Ask a friend if you can practice doing a reading for them. The more you practice, the more comfortable you will become! Ask your friend if they'd like a general reading or if they would prefer a reading based on an area of life, such as love, career, family, etc. Perform different rituals to see what most resonates with you! Here are some examples: lighting a candle before the reading, using sage to cleanse the room, connecting to the energy of your friend before the reading. After the reading, you may ask your friend for some feedback, which can help you improve your skills as you continue to grow.

10.	Discover the Fool's Journey. The Fool's Journey is a metaphor for the journey through life, and the potential challenges and triumphs you'll experience, which are represented in the tarot cards. Lay out all the Major Arcana cards in chronological order. Look to see if you can relate to times in your life where you've experienced the lessons of these cards, beginning with the Fool card and ending with the World card. You may start with the cards chronologically, but it's fine to rearrange the cards to your liking as it relates to your experience. See if the arcs in the Fool's Journey relate to your own life journey. Take note of what you find in this journal!

# Logging the Card Meanings

In the following pages, you'll find space to fill in the following information for each card in your deck:

✳ **Keywords:** An easy way to define each card is to choose a word that resonates with you. These are useful for quick reminders as you create a reference for yourself. Choose three to five keywords to start.

✳ **Correspondences:** Correspondences are other mystical systems that pair well with tarot, for example, numerology, astrology signs, and elements. Taking note of correspondences can be a helpful way to group cards together and reveal additional layers of meaning. See the Tarot Overview Guide (page 9) to see a chart of the correspondences within the tarot deck.

✳ **Reflections:** Use this space to reflect on the messages that come to you as you spend time with the card.

✳ **Reversals:** Use this space to reflect on the messages that come to you when the card is rotated 180 degrees so that it is upside down. Note: Not everyone believes in reading reversals, so only introduce this into your practice if it resonates with you. If you're a beginner, you can start with only upright meanings until you get the hang of it, and then introduce reversals when you're ready. There are many ways you can interpret a reversal, but the two most common ways are to interpret the reversal as the opposite polarity of what the upright card means, or to see it as an impediment or delay of the upright card meaning. Or you can simply tap into your intuition and reflect on whatever message the card is sending you when you view it upside down.

As your tarot journey grows and evolves, you may find that the card's meaning also transforms along with you. Just like any relationship, as you build your relationship to each archetype, putting in the time and effort will allow you to get to know the archetypes of the cards as they are all aspects of you and the human experience. Allow your relationship to each card to evolve and flourish, unveiling more information over time.

# 0. THE FOOL

### REFLECTIONS

_____

_____

_____

_____

_____

### KEYWORDS

_____

_____       _____

_____       _____

_____       _____

_____       _____

### CORRESPONDENCES        ### REVERSALS

_____       _____

_____       _____

_____       _____

_____       _____

_____       _____

# I. THE MAGICIAN

REFLECTIONS

_____

_____

_____

_____

_____

KEYWORDS

_____

_____

_____

_____

CORRESPONDENCES          REVERSALS

_____

_____

_____

_____

# II. THE HIGH PRIESTESS

**REFLECTIONS**

**KEYWORDS**

**CORRESPONDENCES**

**REVERSALS**

# III. THE EMPRESS

## REFLECTIONS

_____
_____
_____
_____
_____

## KEYWORDS

_____
_____
_____
_____
_____

## CORRESPONDENCES

## REVERSALS

_____
_____
_____
_____

# IV. THE EMPEROR

## REFLECTIONS

## KEYWORDS

## CORRESPONDENCES

## REVERSALS

# V. THE HIEROPHANT

## REFLECTIONS

## KEYWORDS

## CORRESPONDENCES

## REVERSALS

# VI. THE LOVERS

### REFLECTIONS

_____

_____

_____

_____

_____

### KEYWORDS

_____

_____

_____

_____

_____

_____

_____

### CORRESPONDENCES

### REVERSALS

_____

_____

_____

_____

_____

_____

_____

_____

# VII. THE CHARIOT

## REFLECTIONS

## KEYWORDS

## CORRESPONDENCES

## REVERSALS

# VIII. STRENGTH

## REFLECTIONS

_____
_____
_____
_____
_____

## KEYWORDS

_____
_____
_____
_____

## CORRESPONDENCES

_____
_____
_____
_____

## REVERSALS

_____
_____
_____
_____

# IX. THE HERMIT

## REFLECTIONS

_____
_____
_____
_____
_____

## KEYWORDS

_____
_____

_____
_____

_____
_____

_____
_____

_____

## CORRESPONDENCES

## REVERSALS

_____
_____

_____
_____

_____
_____

_____
_____

_____
_____

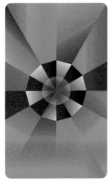

# X. WHEEL OF FORTUNE

## REFLECTIONS

_____

_____

_____

_____

_____

_____

## KEYWORDS

_____

_____

_____

_____

_____

_____

## CORRESPONDENCES

## REVERSALS

_____

_____

_____

_____

_____

_____

_____

_____

# XI. JUSTICE

## REFLECTIONS

## KEYWORDS

## CORRESPONDENCES

## REVERSALS

# XII. THE HANGED WOMAN

### REFLECTIONS

_____

_____

_____

_____

_____

### KEYWORDS

_____  _____

_____  _____

_____  _____

_____  _____

### CORRESPONDENCES   REVERSALS

_____  _____

_____  _____

_____  _____

_____  _____

# XIII. DEATH

## REFLECTIONS

## KEYWORDS

## CORRESPONDENCES

## REVERSALS

# XIV. TEMPERANCE

## REFLECTIONS

_____

_____

_____

_____

## KEYWORDS

_____

_____

_____

_____

## CORRESPONDENCES

_____

_____

_____

_____

## REVERSALS

_____

_____

_____

_____

# XV. THE DEVIL

## REFLECTIONS

_____

_____

_____

_____

## KEYWORDS

_____

_____

_____

_____

_____

## CORRESPONDENCES

## REVERSALS

_____

_____

_____

_____

_____

# XVI. THE TOWER

## REFLECTIONS

## KEYWORDS

## CORRESPONDENCES

## REVERSALS

# XVII. THE STAR

**REFLECTIONS**

_____

_____

_____

_____

_____

_____

**KEYWORDS**

_____

_____

_____

_____

_____

**CORRESPONDENCES**

**REVERSALS**

_____

_____

_____

_____

# XVIII. THE MOON

## REFLECTIONS

_____

_____

_____

_____

_____

## KEYWORDS

_____

_____

_____

_____

_____

## CORRESPONDENCES

_____

_____

_____

_____

_____

## REVERSALS

_____

_____

_____

_____

_____

# XIX. THE SUN

## REFLECTIONS

_____

_____

_____

_____

_____

## KEYWORDS

_____

_____

_____

_____

_____

## CORRESPONDENCES

## REVERSALS

_____

_____

_____

_____

# XX. JUDGEMENT

## REFLECTIONS

_____

_____

_____

_____

_____

## KEYWORDS

_____

_____

_____

_____

_____

_____

## CORRESPONDENCES

## REVERSALS

_____

_____

_____

_____

_____

# XXI. THE WORLD

REFLECTIONS

KEYWORDS

CORRESPONDENCES    REVERSALS

# ACE OF CUPS

### REFLECTIONS

_____

_____

_____

_____

_____

_____

### KEYWORDS

_____

_____       _____

_____       _____

_____       _____

_____       _____

_____

### CORRESPONDENCES        ### REVERSALS

_____       _____

_____       _____

_____       _____

_____       _____

_____       _____

# TWO OF CUPS

## REFLECTIONS

_____

_____

_____

_____

_____

## KEYWORDS

_____

_____

_____

_____

## CORRESPONDENCES

## REVERSALS

_____

_____

_____

_____

# THREE OF CUPS

### REFLECTIONS

_____

_____

_____

_____

_____

### KEYWORDS

_____

_____

_____

_____

_____

_____

_____

_____

_____

### CORRESPONDENCES

### REVERSALS

_____

_____

_____

_____

_____

_____

_____

_____

# FOUR OF CUPS

## REFLECTIONS

_____
_____
_____
_____
_____
_____

## KEYWORDS

_____
_____
_____
_____

## CORRESPONDENCES

_____
_____
_____
_____

## REVERSALS

_____
_____
_____
_____

# FIVE OF CUPS

## REFLECTIONS

## KEYWORDS

## CORRESPONDENCES

## REVERSALS

# SIX OF CUPS

## REFLECTIONS

_____

_____

_____

_____

_____

## KEYWORDS

_____

_____

_____

_____

## CORRESPONDENCES

## REVERSALS

_____

_____

_____

_____

# SEVEN OF CUPS

## REFLECTIONS

_____
_____
_____
_____
_____
_____

## KEYWORDS

_____

_____

_____

_____

## CORRESPONDENCES

_____

_____

_____

_____

## REVERSALS

_____
_____
_____
_____

# EIGHT OF CUPS

## REFLECTIONS

_____
_____
_____
_____
_____

## KEYWORDS

_____
_____
_____
_____
_____

## CORRESPONDENCES

## REVERSALS

_____
_____
_____
_____

# NINE OF CUPS

**REFLECTIONS**

_____

_____

_____

_____

_____

**KEYWORDS**

_____

_____

_____

_____

_____

**CORRESPONDENCES**

**REVERSALS**

_____

_____

_____

_____

# TEN OF CUPS

## REFLECTIONS

_____

_____

_____

_____

_____

_____

## KEYWORDS

_____

_____

_____

_____

## CORRESPONDENCES

_____

_____

_____

_____

## REVERSALS

_____

_____

_____

_____

# PRINCESS OF CUPS

## REFLECTIONS

_____
_____
_____
_____
_____
_____

## KEYWORDS

_____
_____
_____
_____

_____
_____
_____
_____

## CORRESPONDENCES

## REVERSALS

_____
_____
_____
_____

_____
_____
_____
_____

# KNIGHT OF CUPS

## REFLECTIONS

_____

_____

_____

_____

_____

_____

## KEYWORDS

_____

_____

_____

_____

_____

## CORRESPONDENCES

## REVERSALS

_____

_____

_____

_____

_____

# QUEEN OF CUPS

## REFLECTIONS

_____
_____
_____
_____

## KEYWORDS

_____          _____

_____          _____

_____          _____

_____          _____

_____

## CORRESPONDENCES

## REVERSALS

_____          _____

_____          _____

_____          _____

_____          _____

# KING OF CUPS

## REFLECTIONS

_____
_____
_____
_____
_____

## KEYWORDS

_____
_____
_____
_____
_____

## CORRESPONDENCES

_____
_____
_____
_____
_____

## REVERSALS

_____
_____
_____
_____
_____

# ACE OF PENTACLES

## REFLECTIONS

_____

_____

_____

_____

## KEYWORDS

_____

_____

_____

_____

_____

## CORRESPONDENCES

## REVERSALS

_____

_____

_____

_____

# TWO OF PENTACLES

## REFLECTIONS

_____

_____

_____

_____

## KEYWORDS

_____

_____

_____

_____

_____

## CORRESPONDENCES

## REVERSALS

_____

_____

_____

_____

_____

# THREE OF PENTACLES

### REFLECTIONS

_____

_____

_____

_____

_____

### KEYWORDS

_____

_____

_____

_____

### CORRESPONDENCES

### REVERSALS

_____

_____

_____

_____

# FOUR OF PENTACLES

## REFLECTIONS

_____

_____

_____

_____

_____

## KEYWORDS

_____

_____

_____

_____

_____

## CORRESPONDENCES

## REVERSALS

_____

_____

_____

_____

_____

# FIVE OF PENTACLES

## REFLECTIONS

_____

_____

_____

_____

## KEYWORDS

_____

_____

_____

_____

_____

## CORRESPONDENCES

## REVERSALS

_____

_____

_____

_____

_____

# SIX OF PENTACLES

**REFLECTIONS**

_____

_____

_____

_____

_____

**KEYWORDS**

_____

_____

_____

_____

_____

_____

_____

_____

**CORRESPONDENCES**

**REVERSALS**

_____

_____

_____

_____

_____

_____

_____

_____

_____

# SEVEN OF PENTACLES

## REFLECTIONS

_____

_____

_____

_____

_____

_____

## KEYWORDS

_____

_____

_____

_____

## CORRESPONDENCES

## REVERSALS

_____

_____

_____

_____

# EIGHT OF PENTACLES

## REFLECTIONS

_____

_____

_____

_____

_____

## KEYWORDS

_____

_____

_____

_____

## CORRESPONDENCES

_____

_____

_____

_____

## REVERSALS

_____

_____

_____

_____

# NINE OF PENTACLES

REFLECTIONS

_____

_____

_____

_____

_____

_____

KEYWORDS

_____

_____          _____

_____          _____

_____          _____

_____          _____

CORRESPONDENCES          REVERSALS

_____          _____

_____          _____

_____          _____

_____          _____

_____          _____

# TEN OF PENTACLES

## REFLECTIONS

## KEYWORDS

## CORRESPONDENCES

## REVERSALS

# PRINCESS OF PENTACLES

### REFLECTIONS

_____
_____
_____
_____
_____

### KEYWORDS

_____
_____
_____
_____

_____
_____
_____
_____

### CORRESPONDENCES

### REVERSALS

_____
_____
_____
_____

_____
_____
_____
_____

# KNIGHT OF PENTACLES

REFLECTIONS

_____

_____

_____

_____

_____

KEYWORDS

_____

_____            _____

_____            _____

_____            _____

_____            _____

_____

CORRESPONDENCES        REVERSALS

_____            _____

_____            _____

_____            _____

_____            _____

# QUEEN OF PENTACLES

**REFLECTIONS**

_____

_____

_____

_____

_____

**KEYWORDS**

_____

_____

_____

_____

_____

_____

**CORRESPONDENCES**     **REVERSALS**

_____

_____

_____

_____

_____

# KING OF PENTACLES

### REFLECTIONS

_____

_____

_____

_____

_____

### KEYWORDS

_____

_____          _____

_____          _____

_____          _____

_____          _____

### CORRESPONDENCES          ### REVERSALS

_____          _____

_____          _____

_____          _____

_____          _____

# ACE OF SWORDS

### REFLECTIONS

_____

_____

_____

_____

### KEYWORDS

_____

_____

_____

_____

_____

### CORRESPONDENCES

### REVERSALS

_____

_____

_____

_____

# TWO OF SWORDS

## REFLECTIONS

_____

_____

_____

_____

_____

## KEYWORDS

_____

_____

_____

_____

_____

_____

_____

## CORRESPONDENCES

## REVERSALS

_____

_____

_____

_____

# THREE OF SWORDS

REFLECTIONS

_____
_____
_____
_____
_____

KEYWORDS

_____
_____
_____
_____
_____

CORRESPONDENCES        REVERSALS

_____
_____
_____
_____

# FOUR OF SWORDS

## REFLECTIONS

_____

_____

_____

_____

_____

## KEYWORDS

_____

_____

_____

_____

## CORRESPONDENCES

## REVERSALS

_____

_____

_____

_____

_____

# FIVE OF SWORDS

### REFLECTIONS

_____

_____

_____

_____

_____

### KEYWORDS

_____

_____

_____

_____

_____

_____

_____

### CORRESPONDENCES

### REVERSALS

_____

_____

_____

_____

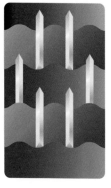

# SIX OF SWORDS

## REFLECTIONS

_____
_____
_____
_____
_____

## KEYWORDS

_____

_____

_____

_____

_____

_____

_____

## CORRESPONDENCES

## REVERSALS

_____

_____

_____

_____

_____

_____

_____

_____

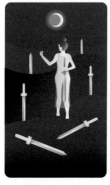

# SEVEN OF SWORDS

## REFLECTIONS

_____

_____

_____

_____

_____

## KEYWORDS

_____

_____

_____

_____

_____

## CORRESPONDENCES

## REVERSALS

_____

_____

_____

_____

_____

# EIGHT OF SWORDS

## REFLECTIONS

_____

_____

_____

_____

## KEYWORDS

_____

_____

_____

_____

_____

## CORRESPONDENCES

## REVERSALS

_____

_____

_____

_____

# NINE OF SWORDS

## REFLECTIONS

_____

_____

_____

_____

_____

## KEYWORDS

_____

_____

_____

_____

_____

_____

_____

## CORRESPONDENCES

## REVERSALS

_____

_____

_____

_____

_____

_____

_____

_____

# TEN OF SWORDS

### REFLECTIONS

_____

_____

_____

_____

### KEYWORDS

_____

_____

_____

_____

_____

### CORRESPONDENCES

### REVERSALS

_____

_____

_____

_____

_____

# PRINCESS OF SWORDS

### REFLECTIONS

### KEYWORDS

### CORRESPONDENCES

### REVERSALS

# KNIGHT OF SWORDS

## REFLECTIONS

_____
_____
_____
_____
_____

## KEYWORDS

_____
_____
_____
_____

## CORRESPONDENCES

_____
_____
_____
_____

## REVERSALS

_____
_____
_____
_____

# QUEEN OF SWORDS

## REFLECTIONS

_____
_____
_____
_____
_____
_____
_____

## KEYWORDS

_____          _____
_____          _____
_____          _____
_____          _____

## CORRESPONDENCES          ## REVERSALS

_____          _____
_____          _____
_____          _____
_____          _____

# KING OF SWORDS

### REFLECTIONS

_____

_____

_____

_____

_____

_____

### KEYWORDS

_____

_____

_____

_____

_____

_____

_____

_____

_____

### CORRESPONDENCES

### REVERSALS

_____

_____

_____

_____

_____

_____

_____

_____

# ACE OF WANDS

## REFLECTIONS

## KEYWORDS

## CORRESPONDENCES

## REVERSALS

# TWO OF WANDS

### REFLECTIONS

_____

_____

_____

_____

_____

### KEYWORDS

_____

_____

_____

_____

_____

_____

_____

_____

### CORRESPONDENCES

### REVERSALS

_____

_____

_____

_____

_____

_____

_____

_____

# THREE OF WANDS

## REFLECTIONS

_____

_____

_____

_____

_____

## KEYWORDS

_____

_____

_____

_____

_____

## CORRESPONDENCES

## REVERSALS

_____

_____

_____

_____

# FOUR OF WANDS

## REFLECTIONS

## KEYWORDS

## CORRESPONDENCES

## REVERSALS

# FIVE OF WANDS

### REFLECTIONS

_____

_____

_____

_____

_____

_____

### KEYWORDS

_____

_____

_____

_____

_____

_____

_____

### CORRESPONDENCES

_____

_____

_____

_____

### REVERSALS

_____

_____

_____

_____

_____

# SIX OF WANDS

**REFLECTIONS**

_____

_____

_____

_____

_____

**KEYWORDS**

_____

_____

_____

_____

_____

**CORRESPONDENCES**     **REVERSALS**

_____

_____

_____

_____

# SEVEN OF WANDS

## REFLECTIONS

## KEYWORDS

## CORRESPONDENCES

## REVERSALS

# EIGHT OF WANDS

## REFLECTIONS

_____
_____
_____
_____
_____

## KEYWORDS

_____
_____
_____
_____

_____
_____
_____
_____

## CORRESPONDENCES

## REVERSALS

_____
_____
_____
_____

_____
_____
_____
_____

# NINE OF WANDS

## REFLECTIONS

_____
_____
_____
_____
_____

## KEYWORDS

_____
_____
_____
_____

## CORRESPONDENCES

_____
_____
_____
_____

## REVERSALS

_____
_____
_____
_____

# TEN OF WANDS

## REFLECTIONS

_____

_____

_____

_____

_____

## KEYWORDS

_____

_____

_____

_____

## CORRESPONDENCES

## REVERSALS

_____

_____

_____

_____

# PRINCESS OF WANDS

## REFLECTIONS

_____
_____
_____
_____
_____

## KEYWORDS

_____
_____
_____
_____
_____

## CORRESPONDENCES

## REVERSALS

_____
_____
_____
_____

# KNIGHT OF WANDS

### REFLECTIONS

_____

_____

_____

_____

_____

### KEYWORDS

_____

_____

_____

_____

_____

_____

### CORRESPONDENCES

### REVERSALS

_____

_____

_____

_____

# QUEEN OF WANDS

## REFLECTIONS

_____

_____

_____

_____

_____

## KEYWORDS

_____

_____

_____

_____

_____

_____

_____

## CORRESPONDENCES

## REVERSALS

_____

_____

_____

_____

_____

_____

_____

_____

# KING OF WANDS

## REFLECTIONS

_____

_____

_____

_____

_____

## KEYWORDS

_____

_____

_____

_____

## CORRESPONDENCES

_____

_____

_____

_____

## REVERSALS

_____

_____

_____

_____

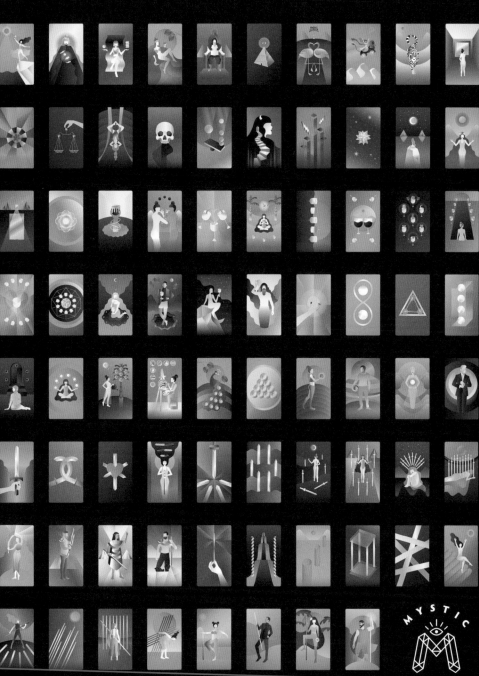

# Card Pairings

You can deepen your relationship to the cards by looking more closely at card pairings. Often, when you see cards alongside one another, new messages and meanings emerge. Practice pulling pairs of cards, and then use the following pages to reflect on what the cards mean to you when paired with one another. Fill in the blank card frames with the names of the cards you're pairing together, then make notes on the reflections and keywords that emerge for you. Take note of the patterns and imagery that come to mind. How do these two cards speak to one another? What story is crafted when the imagery is paired? Note that this may change depending on the context of the reading, for example, a love reading versus a career reading.

REFLECTIONS

KEYWORDS

REFLECTIONS

KEYWORDS

REFLECTIONS

KEYWORDS

**REFLECTIONS**

**KEYWORDS**

**REFLECTIONS**

**KEYWORDS**

**REFLECTIONS**

**KEYWORDS**

REFLECTIONS

KEYWORDS

REFLECTIONS

KEYWORDS

REFLECTIONS

KEYWORDS

REFLECTIONS

KEYWORDS

REFLECTIONS

KEYWORDS

REFLECTIONS

KEYWORDS

**REFLECTIONS**

**KEYWORDS**

**REFLECTIONS**

**KEYWORDS**

**REFLECTIONS**

**KEYWORDS**

REFLECTIONS

KEYWORDS

REFLECTIONS

KEYWORDS

REFLECTIONS

KEYWORDS

**REFLECTIONS**

**KEYWORDS**

**REFLECTIONS**

**KEYWORDS**

**REFLECTIONS**

**KEYWORDS**

REFLECTIONS

KEYWORDS

REFLECTIONS

KEYWORDS

REFLECTIONS

KEYWORDS

REFLECTIONS

KEYWORDS

REFLECTIONS

KEYWORDS

REFLECTIONS

KEYWORDS

REFLECTIONS

_____

_____

_____

_____

KEYWORDS

_____

_____

_____

REFLECTIONS

_____

_____

_____

_____

KEYWORDS

_____

_____

_____

REFLECTIONS

_____

_____

_____

_____

KEYWORDS

_____

_____

_____

REFLECTIONS

KEYWORDS

REFLECTIONS

KEYWORDS

REFLECTIONS

KEYWORDS

REFLECTIONS

KEYWORDS

REFLECTIONS

KEYWORDS

REFLECTIONS

KEYWORDS

**REFLECTIONS**

**KEYWORDS**

**REFLECTIONS**

**KEYWORDS**

**REFLECTIONS**

**KEYWORDS**

**REFLECTIONS**

**KEYWORDS**

**REFLECTIONS**

**KEYWORDS**

**REFLECTIONS**

**KEYWORDS**

REFLECTIONS

KEYWORDS

REFLECTIONS

KEYWORDS

REFLECTIONS

KEYWORDS

**REFLECTIONS**

**KEYWORDS**

**REFLECTIONS**

**KEYWORDS**

**REFLECTIONS**

**KEYWORDS**

REFLECTIONS

_____

KEYWORDS

_____

REFLECTIONS

_____

KEYWORDS

_____

REFLECTIONS

_____

KEYWORDS

_____

REFLECTIONS

KEYWORDS

REFLECTIONS

KEYWORDS

REFLECTIONS

KEYWORDS

REFLECTIONS

KEYWORDS

REFLECTIONS

KEYWORDS

REFLECTIONS

KEYWORDS

**REFLECTIONS**

**KEYWORDS**

**REFLECTIONS**

**KEYWORDS**

**REFLECTIONS**

**KEYWORDS**

REFLECTIONS

KEYWORDS

REFLECTIONS

KEYWORDS

REFLECTIONS

KEYWORDS

VIII. STRENGTH

# Tarot Spreads

A tarot spread is a layout of multiple tarot cards. Each card in the spread is assigned significance based on where it is placed, which gives the cards context for what they mean in relation to one another. The order the cards are pulled and the position they hold in the spread all contain meaning.

Within the world of tarot, you can always find a tarot spread that suits your needs. Whether it's a spread you like to use during the full moon or a spread related to romance, there is always an opportunity to pull cards whenever you fancy! In this section, you'll find two sample spreads created by Mystic Mondays to help get you started; the remaining spreads are blank for you to fill in. You can record favorite spreads that you've learned from other tarot readers so you can easily reference them whenever you need them, and you'll also have the opportunity to create your own custom spreads.

The layouts include space to record the following:

∗  **Title:** The name of the spread

∗  **Source:** The physical or digital resource and creator of the spread

∗  **Sketch:** Space to draw your spread

∗  **Meaning:** The card position prompt

# How to Create Your Own Tarot Spreads

To begin creating your own tarot spread, consider a problem you'd like to solve or a question you'd like answered. Then design a spread that will help you receive the messages you're looking for.

You can also draw inspiration from existing spreads—take note of what some of your favorite tarot spreads have in common, and you can infuse those elements into the new spreads you create.

To create your own spread:

* Ask yourself, "What is the theme?" Consider choosing a theme for your spread. For example, you could create a spread that uses moon phases, or a spread related to an area of life, like career or love.

* Consider what you want to know from the deck and come up with questions. Once you've determined what you want the deck to answer, think of at least three introspective questions that can enhance your self-awareness around your main query. Ask open-ended questions rather than "yes" or "no" questions.

For example, if your main query is "What guidance do I need to enhance my spiritual growth?" here are three questions you might ask:

* *What are my natural gifts when it comes to my spiritual growth?*

* *What is potentially blocking me from moving forward?*

* *What is my desired outcome when it comes to my spiritual growth?*

Consider contrasts so that the querent (the person asking the question) can understand the big picture. Examples: light versus dark, positive versus negative.

✳ **Finesse your questions:** Look at the questions you'd like to ask and think of how you can ask those questions in different ways. Notice how reframing the questions impacts your perspective.

✳ **Choose a layout:** When designing the layout of your spread—the order in which you select and display the cards—think about the relationship between the cards and what story they create when read in the order you've outlined. For example, most people read from left to right, so consider how most people would approach the spread naturally, without any instruction to do so. Based on the prompts of each placement, ask yourself what you're hoping the querent will receive from asking and answering these questions.

As you become more comfortable creating your own spreads, you might consider the following elements:

✳ *Will you use a significator card to represent the querent?*

✳ *If cards in your spread overlap—for example, in the shape of a cross—what is the relationship between the cards that touch?*

✳ *Do you want to use supporting elements like numerology within your spread?*

✳ *How will the layout of your spread support the question being asked?*

✳ *How will the layout of your spread indicate the theme?*

# SPREAD TITLE

**SOURCE**

**CARD MEANINGS**

1.

2.

3.

4.

5.

6.

7.

8.

9.

10.

11.

12.

13.

14.

15.

16.

17.

18.

19.

20.

# SPREAD TITLE

SOURCE

CARD MEANINGS

1.

2.

3.

4.

5.

6.

7.

8.

9.

10.

11.

12.

13.

14.

15.

16.

17.

18.

19.

20.

# SPREAD TITLE

SOURCE

CARD MEANINGS

1.

2.

3.

4.

5.

6.

7.

8.

9.

10.

11.

12.

13.

14.

15.

16.

17.

18.

19.

20.

# SPREAD TITLE

SOURCE

CARD MEANINGS

1.

2.

3.

4.

5.

6.

7.

8.

9.

10.

11.

12.

13.

14.

15.

16.

17.

18.

19.

20.

# SPREAD TITLE

**SOURCE**

**CARD MEANINGS**

1.

2.

3.

4.

5.

6.

7.

8.

9.

10.

11.

12.

13.

14.

15.

16.

17.

18.

19.

20.

# SPREAD TITLE

SOURCE

CARD MEANINGS

1.

2.

3.

4.

5.

6.

7.

8.

9.

10.

11.

12.

13.

14.

15.

16.

17.

18.

19.

20.

# SPREAD TITLE

SOURCE

CARD MEANINGS

1.

2.

3.

4.

5.

6.

7.

8.

9.

10.

11.

12.

13.

14.

15.

16.

17.

18.

19.

20.

# SPREAD TITLE

SOURCE

CARD MEANINGS

1.

2.

3.

4.

5.

6.

7.

8.

9.

10.

11.

12.

13.

14.

15.

16.

17.

18.

19.

20.

# SPREAD TITLE

SOURCE

CARD MEANINGS

1.

2.

3.

4.

5.

6.

7.

8.

9.

10.

11.

12.

13.

14.

15.

16.

17.

18.

19.

20.

# SPREAD TITLE

SOURCE

CARD MEANINGS

1.

2.

3.

4.

5.

6.

7.

8.

9.

10.

11.

12.

13.

14.

15.

16.

17.

18.

19.

20.

# SPREAD TITLE

SOURCE

CARD MEANINGS

1.

2.

3.

4.

5.

6.

7.

8.

9.

10.

11.

12.

13.

14.

15.

16.

17.

18.

19.

20.

# SPREAD TITLE

**SOURCE**

**CARD MEANINGS**

1.

2.

3.

4.

5.

6.

7.

8.

9.

10.

11.

12.

13.

14.

15.

16.

17.

18.

19.

20.

# SPREAD TITLE

SOURCE

CARD MEANINGS

1.

2.

3.

4.

5.

6.

7.

8.

9.

10.

11.

12.

13.

14.

15.

16.

17.

18.

19.

20.

# SPREAD TITLE

SOURCE

CARD MEANINGS

1.

2.

3.

4.

5.

6.

7.

8.

9.

10.

11.

12.

13.

14.

15.

16.

17.

18.

19.

20.

# SPREAD TITLE

SOURCE

CARD MEANINGS

1.

2.

3.

4.

5.

6.

7.

8.

9.

10.

11.

12.

13.

14.

15.

16.

17.

18.

19.

20.

II. HIGH PRIESTESS

# Tarot Readings

In this section, you'll discover space to record your tarot readings, including readings you perform for yourself, readings you perform for others, and readings you receive from other tarot readers.

Reading tarot is a practice that combines your intuition, knowledge, and senses. When you're reading for yourself (which is how most people start), it allows you to access your inner voice that may not always get a chance to truly speak to you with all the distractions from the outside world. The more you practice tarot readings, the more you will gain confidence in your abilities as a tarot reader and develop your own unique style of reading cards in a way that no one else can. In time, when you read for others, you'll find words coming out of your mouth that make perfect sense to the person you're reading for, based on the cards that were pulled.

As you continue your journey of tarot reading, be open to different methods, techniques, and perspectives. You may want to pair your practice with other resources like books, podcasts, and courses. Absorbing a range of information will help you define your own style of tarot reading and discover what feels the most authentic to you. Allow yourself to experiment with different rituals like shuffling, pulling cards, incantations, intention setting, and journaling. As you change and grow, you may see your tarot practice evolve too!

# Logging Your Tarot Readings

Each spread in this section includes space to record the following:

✳ **Querent:** The person asking the question (this could be you or another person)

✳ **Date:** Tracking the date and if it is a significant time, like during a moon phase

✳ **Location:** The influence of the environment can influence the reading and help you remember what the reading said.

✳ **Question:** The question that was asked of the deck. Remember, tarot is most effective when open-ended questions are asked. Avoid asking yes or no questions.

✳ **Spread:** Space to record the name of the spread you followed

✳ **Moon phase:** Icons showing the moon phases—circle the phase that the moon was in when the reading was done.

✳ **Interpretation:** Use this space to record any significant thoughts, reflections, or revelations.

✳ **Blank space:** An open grid to sketch the cards you pulled

As you practice logging and reflecting on your tarot readings, you'll begin to see patterns emerge between the cards and the messages within the spreads. As you continue to log your readings, you can always look back on the reading to see how accurately the cards responded to your question. When you give yourself space and time, you allow yourself to get a different perspective. Perhaps your reading doesn't completely resonate with you at first. A month later you can go back to that reading, and it might make more sense. Don't pressure yourself to have all the answers. As you develop your relationship with the cards, also take note of your moods during readings. How you approach a reading is often the energy that is reflected back at you! Be open to the process as you journal your findings.

QUERENT _____  DATE _____

LOCATION _____  DECK _____

QUESTION _____  SPREAD _____

_____  MOON PHASE ○ ☽ ◐ ◑ ● ◐ ◑ ☾

\*   \*   \*   \*   \*   \*   \*   \*   \*   \*

\*   \*   \*   \*   \*   \*   \*   \*   \*   \*

\*   \*   \*   \*   \*   \*   \*   \*   \*   \*

\*   \*   \*   \*   \*   \*   \*   \*   \*   \*

\*   \*   \*   \*   \*   \*   \*   \*   \*   \*

\*   \*   \*   \*   \*   \*   \*   \*   \*   \*

\*   \*   \*   \*   \*   \*   \*   \*   \*   \*

\*   \*   \*   \*   \*   \*   \*   \*   \*   \*

\*   \*   \*   \*   \*   \*   \*   \*   \*   \*

\*   \*   \*   \*   \*   \*   \*   \*   \*   \*

\*   \*   \*   \*   \*   \*   \*   \*   \*   \*

\*   \*   \*   \*   \*   \*   \*   \*   \*   \*

# 👁 INTERPRETATION

QUERENT _____  DATE _____

LOCATION _____  DECK _____

QUESTION _____  SPREAD _____

_____  MOON PHASE ○ ☽ ◑ ◑ ● ◐ ◐ ☾

## 👁 INTERPRETATION

QUERENT _____  DATE _____

LOCATION _____  DECK _____

QUESTION _____  SPREAD _____

_____  MOON PHASE ○ ◗ ◖ ◕ ● ◑ ◐ ☾

\* \* \* \* \* \* \* \* \* \*

\* \* \* \* \* \* \* \* \* \*

\* \* \* \* \* \* \* \* \* \*

\* \* \* \* \* \* \* \* \* \*

\* \* \* \* \* \* \* \* \* \*

\* \* \* \* \* \* \* \* \* \*

\* \* \* \* \* \* \* \* \* \*

\* \* \* \* \* \* \* \* \* \*

\* \* \* \* \* \* \* \* \* \*

\* \* \* \* \* \* \* \* \* \*

\* \* \* \* \* \* \* \* \* \*

\* \* \* \* \* \* \* \* \* \*

# 👁 INTERPRETATION

QUERENT _____  DATE _____

LOCATION _____  DECK _____

QUESTION _____  SPREAD _____

_____  MOON PHASE ○ ☽ ◑ ◐ ● ◑ ◐ ☾

\* \* \* \* \* \* \* \* \* \*

\* \* \* \* \* \* \* \* \* \*

\* \* \* \* \* \* \* \* \* \*

\* \* \* \* \* \* \* \* \* \*

\* \* \* \* \* \* \* \* \* \*

\* \* \* \* \* \* \* \* \* \*

\* \* \* \* \* \* \* \* \* \*

\* \* \* \* \* \* \* \* \* \*

\* \* \* \* \* \* \* \* \* \*

\* \* \* \* \* \* \* \* \* \*

\* \* \* \* \* \* \* \* \* \*

\* \* \* \* \* \* \* \* \* \*

# 👁 INTERPRETATION

QUERENT _____     DATE _____

LOCATION _____     DECK _____

QUESTION _____     SPREAD _____

_____     MOON PHASE ○ ☽ ◐ ◑ ● ◑ ◐ ☾

\* \* \* \* \*      \* \* \* \* \*

\* \* \* \* \*      \* \* \* \* \*

\* \* \* \* \*      \* \* \* \* \*

\* \* \* \* \*      \* \* \* \* \*

\* \* \* \* \*      \* \* \* \* \*

\* \* \* \* \*      \* \* \* \* \*

\* \* \* \* \*      \* \* \* \* \*

\* \* \* \* \*      \* \* \* \* \*

\* \* \* \* \*      \* \* \* \* \*

\* \* \* \* \*      \* \* \* \* \*

\* \* \* \* \*      \* \* \* \* \*

\* \* \* \* \*      \* \* \* \* \*

## 👁 INTERPRETATION

QUERENT _____   DATE _____

LOCATION _____   DECK _____

QUESTION _____   SPREAD _____

_____   MOON PHASE ○ ☽ ◑ ◐ ● ◕ ◑ ☾

| | | | | | | | | | |
|---|---|---|---|---|---|---|---|---|---|
| * | * | * | * | * | * | * | * | * | * |
| * | * | * | * | * | * | * | * | * | * |
| * | * | * | * | * | * | * | * | * | * |
| * | * | * | * | * | * | * | * | * | * |
| * | * | * | * | * | * | * | * | * | * |
| * | * | * | * | * | * | * | * | * | * |
| * | * | * | * | * | * | * | * | * | * |
| * | * | * | * | * | * | * | * | * | * |
| * | * | * | * | * | * | * | * | * | * |
| * | * | * | * | * | * | * | * | * | * |
| * | * | * | * | * | * | * | * | * | * |
| * | * | * | * | * | * | * | * | * | * |

## 👁 INTERPRETATION

QUERENT _____     DATE _____

LOCATION _____     DECK _____

QUESTION _____     SPREAD _____

_____     MOON PHASE ○ ☽ ◐ ◑ ● ◑ ◐ ☾

\*   \*   \*   \*   \*   \*   \*   \*   \*   \*

\*   \*   \*   \*   \*   \*   \*   \*   \*   \*

\*   \*   \*   \*   \*   \*   \*   \*   \*   \*

\*   \*   \*   \*   \*   \*   \*   \*   \*   \*

\*   \*   \*   \*   \*   \*   \*   \*   \*   \*

\*   \*   \*   \*   \*   \*   \*   \*   \*   \*

\*   \*   \*   \*   \*   \*   \*   \*   \*   \*

\*   \*   \*   \*   \*   \*   \*   \*   \*   \*

\*   \*   \*   \*   \*   \*   \*   \*   \*   \*

\*   \*   \*   \*   \*   \*   \*   \*   \*   \*

\*   \*   \*   \*   \*   \*   \*   \*   \*   \*

\*   \*   \*   \*   \*   \*   \*   \*   \*   \*

## 👁 INTERPRETATION

QUERENT _____     DATE _____

LOCATION _____     DECK _____

QUESTION _____     SPREAD _____

_____     MOON PHASE ○ ☽ ◑ ◑ ● ◐ ◐ ☾

\*   \*   \*   \*   \*   \*   \*   \*   \*   \*

\*   \*   \*   \*   \*   \*   \*   \*   \*   \*

\*   \*   \*   \*   \*   \*   \*   \*   \*   \*

\*   \*   \*   \*   \*   \*   \*   \*   \*   \*

\*   \*   \*   \*   \*   \*   \*   \*   \*   \*

\*   \*   \*   \*   \*   \*   \*   \*   \*   \*

\*   \*   \*   \*   \*   \*   \*   \*   \*   \*

\*   \*   \*   \*   \*   \*   \*   \*   \*   \*

\*   \*   \*   \*   \*   \*   \*   \*   \*   \*

\*   \*   \*   \*   \*   \*   \*   \*   \*   \*

\*   \*   \*   \*   \*   \*   \*   \*   \*   \*

\*   \*   \*   \*   \*   \*   \*   \*   \*   \*

# 👁 INTERPRETATION

QUERENT _____    DATE _____

LOCATION _____    DECK _____

QUESTION _____    SPREAD _____

_____    MOON PHASE ○ ☽ ◑ ◐ ● ◐ ◑ ☾

# 👁 INTERPRETATION

QUERENT _____     DATE _____

LOCATION _____     DECK _____

QUESTION _____     SPREAD _____

_____     MOON PHASE ○ ) ◐ ◑ ● ◑ ◐ ☾

\*  \*  \*  \*  \*    \*  \*  \*  \*  \*

\*  \*  \*  \*  \*    \*  \*  \*  \*  \*

\*  \*  \*  \*  \*    \*  \*  \*  \*  \*

\*  \*  \*  \*  \*    \*  \*  \*  \*  \*

\*  \*  \*  \*  \*    \*  \*  \*  \*  \*

\*  \*  \*  \*  \*    \*  \*  \*  \*  \*

\*  \*  \*  \*  \*    \*  \*  \*  \*  \*

\*  \*  \*  \*  \*    \*  \*  \*  \*  \*

\*  \*  \*  \*  \*    \*  \*  \*  \*  \*

\*  \*  \*  \*  \*    \*  \*  \*  \*  \*

\*  \*  \*  \*  \*    \*  \*  \*  \*  \*

\*  \*  \*  \*  \*    \*  \*  \*  \*  \*

## 👁 INTERPRETATION

QUERENT _____

LOCATION _____

QUESTION _____

_____

DATE _____

DECK _____

SPREAD _____

MOON PHASE ○ ) ◐ ◑ ● ◐ ◑ ☾

\*  \*  \*  \*  \*  \*  \*  \*  \*  \*

\*  \*  \*  \*  \*  \*  \*  \*  \*  \*

\*  \*  \*  \*  \*  \*  \*  \*  \*  \*

\*  \*  \*  \*  \*  \*  \*  \*  \*  \*

\*  \*  \*  \*  \*  \*  \*  \*  \*  \*

\*  \*  \*  \*  \*  \*  \*  \*  \*  \*

\*  \*  \*  \*  \*  \*  \*  \*  \*  \*

\*  \*  \*  \*  \*  \*  \*  \*  \*  \*

\*  \*  \*  \*  \*  \*  \*  \*  \*  \*

\*  \*  \*  \*  \*  \*  \*  \*  \*  \*

\*  \*  \*  \*  \*  \*  \*  \*  \*  \*

\*  \*  \*  \*  \*  \*  \*  \*  \*  \*

## 👁 INTERPRETATION

QUERENT _____     DATE _____

LOCATION _____     DECK _____

QUESTION _____     SPREAD _____

_____     MOON PHASE ○ ☽ ◑ ◕ ● ◕ ◐ ☾

## 👁 INTERPRETATION

QUERENT _____    DATE _____

LOCATION _____    DECK _____

QUESTION _____    SPREAD _____

_____    MOON PHASE ○ ☽ ◐ ◑ ● ◑ ☾

\* \* \* \* \* \* \* \* \* \*

\* \* \* \* \* \* \* \* \* \*

\* \* \* \* \* \* \* \* \* \*

\* \* \* \* \* \* \* \* \* \*

\* \* \* \* \* \* \* \* \* \*

\* \* \* \* \* \* \* \* \* \*

\* \* \* \* \* \* \* \* \* \*

\* \* \* \* \* \* \* \* \* \*

\* \* \* \* \* \* \* \* \* \*

\* \* \* \* \* \* \* \* \* \*

\* \* \* \* \* \* \* \* \* \*

\* \* \* \* \* \* \* \* \* \*

## 👁 INTERPRETATION

QUERENT _____     DATE _____

LOCATION _____    DECK _____

QUESTION _____    SPREAD _____

_____             MOON PHASE ○ ) ◗ ◖ ● ◐ ◑ ☾

＊ ＊ ＊ ＊ ＊ ＊ ＊ ＊ ＊ ＊

＊ ＊ ＊ ＊ ＊ ＊ ＊ ＊ ＊ ＊

＊ ＊ ＊ ＊ ＊ ＊ ＊ ＊ ＊ ＊

＊ ＊ ＊ ＊ ＊ ＊ ＊ ＊ ＊ ＊

＊ ＊ ＊ ＊ ＊ ＊ ＊ ＊ ＊ ＊

＊ ＊ ＊ ＊ ＊ ＊ ＊ ＊ ＊ ＊

＊ ＊ ＊ ＊ ＊ ＊ ＊ ＊ ＊ ＊

＊ ＊ ＊ ＊ ＊ ＊ ＊ ＊ ＊ ＊

＊ ＊ ＊ ＊ ＊ ＊ ＊ ＊ ＊ ＊

＊ ＊ ＊ ＊ ＊ ＊ ＊ ＊ ＊ ＊

＊ ＊ ＊ ＊ ＊ ＊ ＊ ＊ ＊ ＊

＊ ＊ ＊ ＊ ＊ ＊ ＊ ＊ ＊ ＊

# 👁 INTERPRETATION

QUERENT _____     DATE _____

LOCATION _____     DECK _____

QUESTION _____     SPREAD _____

_____     MOON PHASE ○ ☽ ◐ ◑ ● ◑ ◐ ☾

## 👁 INTERPRETATION

QUERENT _____  DATE _____

LOCATION _____  DECK _____

QUESTION _____  SPREAD _____

_____  MOON PHASE ○ ) ◑ ◐ ● ◑ ◗ ☾

# 👁 INTERPRETATION

QUERENT _____ DATE _____

LOCATION _____ DECK _____

QUESTION _____ SPREAD _____

_____ MOON PHASE ○ ☽ ◗ ◑ ● ◐ ◑ ☾

# 👁 INTERPRETATION

QUERENT _____    DATE _____

LOCATION _____    DECK _____

QUESTION _____    SPREAD _____

_____    MOON PHASE ○ ☽ ◐ ◑ ● ◑ ◐ ☾

\* \* \* \* \* \* \* \* \* \*

\* \* \* \* \* \* \* \* \* \*

\* \* \* \* \* \* \* \* \* \*

\* \* \* \* \* \* \* \* \* \*

\* \* \* \* \* \* \* \* \* \*

\* \* \* \* \* \* \* \* \* \*

\* \* \* \* \* \* \* \* \* \*

\* \* \* \* \* \* \* \* \* \*

\* \* \* \* \* \* \* \* \* \*

\* \* \* \* \* \* \* \* \* \*

\* \* \* \* \* \* \* \* \* \*

\* \* \* \* \* \* \* \* \* \*

## 👁 INTERPRETATION

QUERENT _____   DATE _____

LOCATION _____   DECK _____

QUESTION _____   SPREAD _____

_____   MOON PHASE ○ ☽ ◖ ◕ ● ◑ ◗ ☾

\* \* \* \* \*     \* \* \* \* \*

\* \* \* \* \*     \* \* \* \* \*

\* \* \* \* \*     \* \* \* \* \*

\* \* \* \* \*     \* \* \* \* \*

\* \* \* \* \*     \* \* \* \* \*

\* \* \* \* \*     \* \* \* \* \*

\* \* \* \* \*     \* \* \* \* \*

\* \* \* \* \*     \* \* \* \* \*

\* \* \* \* \*     \* \* \* \* \*

\* \* \* \* \*     \* \* \* \* \*

\* \* \* \* \*     \* \* \* \* \*

\* \* \* \* \*     \* \* \* \* \*

## 👁 INTERPRETATION

QUERENT _____     DATE _____

LOCATION _____     DECK _____

QUESTION _____     SPREAD _____

_____     MOON PHASE ○ ☽ ◑ ◕ ● ◑ ◐ ☾

\*  \*  \*  \*  \*  \*  \*  \*  \*  \*

\*  \*  \*  \*  \*  \*  \*  \*  \*  \*

\*  \*  \*  \*  \*  \*  \*  \*  \*  \*

\*  \*  \*  \*  \*  \*  \*  \*  \*  \*

\*  \*  \*  \*  \*  \*  \*  \*  \*  \*

\*  \*  \*  \*  \*  \*  \*  \*  \*  \*

\*  \*  \*  \*  \*  \*  \*  \*  \*  \*

\*  \*  \*  \*  \*  \*  \*  \*  \*  \*

\*  \*  \*  \*  \*  \*  \*  \*  \*  \*

\*  \*  \*  \*  \*  \*  \*  \*  \*  \*

\*  \*  \*  \*  \*  \*  \*  \*  \*  \*

\*  \*  \*  \*  \*  \*  \*  \*  \*  \*

## 👁 INTERPRETATION

XV. THE DEVIL

# Tarot Tools & Resources

Use this space to build your own tarot library! In this section you can record your favorite tarot tools and resources, including your tarot deck collection, your tarot community, and your favorite digital and physical resources.

## Tarot Decks

Every tarot deck has its own personality and each deck is infused with the personality of the creator, with ways of relaying messages that can speak to you like a friend would. Lucky for us, there are many tarot and oracle decks to choose from and to add to our collections! As tarot and oracle decks become more popular, more creators are designing decks based on their own experiences and unique lenses on life—whether these decks reference their heritage, spiritual beliefs, or whatnot, we can most likely find a deck that we can work with that also resonates and speaks to us. We can amass a multitude of decks to be used in our practice at varying times!

Use this space to track the decks you have, the decks you want, and the ones you've outgrown (or passed along to a friend). This can be a great way to inventory all the decks you have or have had in your collection.

| NAME | AUTHOR | WISH LIST | OWNED | RECOMMENDED | OUTGROWN | GIFTED |
|------|--------|-----------|-------|-------------|----------|--------|
| | | ☐ | ☐ | ☐ | ☐ | ☐ |
| | | ☐ | ☐ | ☐ | ☐ | ☐ |
| | | ☐ | ☐ | ☐ | ☐ | ☐ |
| | | ☐ | ☐ | ☐ | ☐ | ☐ |
| | | ☐ | ☐ | ☐ | ☐ | ☐ |
| | | ☐ | ☐ | ☐ | ☐ | ☐ |
| | | ☐ | ☐ | ☐ | ☐ | ☐ |
| | | ☐ | ☐ | ☐ | ☐ | ☐ |
| | | ☐ | ☐ | ☐ | ☐ | ☐ |
| | | ☐ | ☐ | ☐ | ☐ | ☐ |
| | | ☐ | ☐ | ☐ | ☐ | ☐ |
| | | ☐ | ☐ | ☐ | ☐ | ☐ |
| | | ☐ | ☐ | ☐ | ☐ | ☐ |
| | | ☐ | ☐ | ☐ | ☐ | ☐ |
| | | ☐ | ☐ | ☐ | ☐ | ☐ |
| | | ☐ | ☐ | ☐ | ☐ | ☐ |
| | | ☐ | ☐ | ☐ | ☐ | ☐ |
| | | ☐ | ☐ | ☐ | ☐ | ☐ |
| | | ☐ | ☐ | ☐ | ☐ | ☐ |
| | | ☐ | ☐ | ☐ | ☐ | ☐ |
| | | ☐ | ☐ | ☐ | ☐ | ☐ |

| NAME | AUTHOR | WISH LIST | OWNED | RECOMMENDED | OUTGROWN | GIFTED |
|------|--------|-----------|-------|-------------|----------|--------|
| | | ☐ | ☐ | ☐ | ☐ | ☐ |
| | | ☐ | ☐ | ☐ | ☐ | ☐ |
| | | ☐ | ☐ | ☐ | ☐ | ☐ |
| | | ☐ | ☐ | ☐ | ☐ | ☐ |
| | | ☐ | ☐ | ☐ | ☐ | ☐ |
| | | ☐ | ☐ | ☐ | ☐ | ☐ |
| | | ☐ | ☐ | ☐ | ☐ | ☐ |
| | | ☐ | ☐ | ☐ | ☐ | ☐ |
| | | ☐ | ☐ | ☐ | ☐ | ☐ |
| | | ☐ | ☐ | ☐ | ☐ | ☐ |
| | | ☐ | ☐ | ☐ | ☐ | ☐ |
| | | ☐ | ☐ | ☐ | ☐ | ☐ |
| | | ☐ | ☐ | ☐ | ☐ | ☐ |
| | | ☐ | ☐ | ☐ | ☐ | ☐ |
| | | ☐ | ☐ | ☐ | ☐ | ☐ |
| | | ☐ | ☐ | ☐ | ☐ | ☐ |
| | | ☐ | ☐ | ☐ | ☐ | ☐ |
| | | ☐ | ☐ | ☐ | ☐ | ☐ |
| | | ☐ | ☐ | ☐ | ☐ | ☐ |
| | | ☐ | ☐ | ☐ | ☐ | ☐ |
| | | ☐ | ☐ | ☐ | ☐ | ☐ |

# Tarot Deck Interview

Interviewing your decks is a lovely way to get to know each deck in your collection. Receiving a new deck is like starting a new relationship, as each deck contains its own personality. To check the vibe between you and your deck, you can conduct a tarot deck interview as a way of introducing yourselves to each other. Engaging with the deck will allow you to recognize its strengths and weaknesses, and will give you a clear sense of occasion and what it might be best used for.

The following pages include space for you to record your deck interviews. Having all your deck interviews in one place can help you compare and contrast your different decks' powers. Use this interview spread as an initiation and to better understand how you can use this deck, what circumstances this deck is best used in, and how this deck likes to communicate. Pull a card in response to each of the seven questions listed below, and lay them out following the seven-card spread shown on the facing page.

1.    What is the energy of this deck?

2.    How can this deck best support me?

3.    What is this deck's strengths?

4.    What is this deck's weakness?

5.    In what realm will we best communicate?

6.    How will our relationship develop?

7.    What guidance can you offer me at this moment?

## 👁 DECK INTERVIEW REFLECTION

## 👁 DECK INTERVIEW REFLECTION

# 👁 DECK INTERVIEW REFLECTION

## 👁 DECK INTERVIEW REFLECTION

## 👁 DECK INTERVIEW REFLECTION

## 👁 DECK INTERVIEW REFLECTION

## 👁 DECK INTERVIEW REFLECTION

## 👁 DECK INTERVIEW REFLECTION

## 👁 DECK INTERVIEW REFLECTION

# 👁️ DECK INTERVIEW REFLECTION

# Tarot Coven

Use the space below to keep track of your tarot coven—people in your in-person and digital tarot communities. This could include friends who read tarot, people who have done readings for you, readers you hope to collaborate with, and readers you follow online.

Mystic Mondays also has an online community of tarot readers. Join us at www.coven.mysticmondays.com.

NAME

SOCIAL HANDLE(S)

WEBSITE

FAVORITE DECKS


NAME

SOCIAL HANDLE(S)

WEBSITE

FAVORITE DECKS

NAME

SOCIAL HANDLE(S)

WEBSITE

FAVORITE DECKS


NAME

SOCIAL HANDLE(S)

WEBSITE

FAVORITE DECKS


NAME

SOCIAL HANDLE(S)

WEBSITE

FAVORITE DECKS


NAME

SOCIAL HANDLE(S)

WEBSITE

FAVORITE DECKS

NAME

SOCIAL HANDLE(S)

WEBSITE

FAVORITE DECKS

NAME

SOCIAL HANDLE(S)

WEBSITE

FAVORITE DECKS

NAME

SOCIAL HANDLE(S)

WEBSITE

FAVORITE DECKS

NAME

SOCIAL HANDLE(S)

WEBSITE

FAVORITE DECKS

NAME

SOCIAL HANDLE(S)

WEBSITE

FAVORITE DECKS


NAME

SOCIAL HANDLE(S)

WEBSITE

FAVORITE DECKS


NAME

SOCIAL HANDLE(S)

WEBSITE

FAVORITE DECKS


NAME

SOCIAL HANDLE(S)

WEBSITE

FAVORITE DECKS

# Powerful and Insightful Tarot Resources

Learning from those who have shared and taught before us is a beautiful way to grow a tarot practice. This section allows you to keep track of physical and digital resources such as books, social media accounts, and other inspirational metaphysical resources—including tarot, astrology, numerology, and other magical modalities that enhance your learning.

Here are a few Mystic Mondays resources to get you started:

* Visit www.mysticmondays.com for a variety of powerful tarot resources

* Join our online community at www.coven.mysticmondays.com

* Download the Mystic Mondays app and draw your tarot and oracle cards on the go!

* Follow Mystic Mondays on social media at @mysticmondays